On Track To FIRST GRADE

Written by
Alex Cleveland
Barb Caton

Art by
David Jensen
Carol Koeller

38W567 Brindlewood Elgin, Illinois 60123

ART:

Cover
> David Jensen
> Chicago, Illinois

Text
> Carol Koeller
> Chicago, Illinois

Text and Graphics Layout
> David Jensen
> Chicago, Illinois

Photograph
> Autumn Pettibone

© 2002 Liz and Dick Wilmes

ISBN 0-943452-32-5
Printed in the United States of America.

PUBLISHED BY:

38W567 Brindlewood
Elgin, Illinois 60123

DISTRIBUTED BY:

Gryphon House
P.O. Box 207
Beltsville, MD 20704

(Educational Stores & Catalogues)

Consortium Book Sales
1045 Westgate Drive
St. Paul, MN 55114

(U.S. Book Trade)

Monarch Books
5000 Dufferin St., Unit K
Downsview, Ontario
Canada M3H 5T5

(All Canadian Orders)

DISCLAIMER: The publisher and authors cannot be held responsible for injury, mishap, or damages incurred during the use of or because of the activities in this book. The authors recommend appropriate and reasonable supervision at all times based on the age and capability of each child.

DEDICATED TO:

All the parents who encouraged us to write this book. We appreciate your support and commitment to helping your children continue learning at home.

Special thanks to:

Mom, Dad, Adlai Jr., Cody, Autumn, and Coral
Dick, Kevin, Meghan, Cliff, and Walker

Biography

Barb and Alex have Master's degrees in Education plus Early Childhood endorsements. Each has taught young children for twenty-seven years. They are the co-authors of **ACTIVITIES UNLIMITED, GAMES FOR ALL SEASONS** and **On Track To KINDERGARTEN**. Drawing on their vast experience and knowledge of sensory motor development they are active presenters at early childhood conferences.

Table of Contents

DEAR TEACHERS

On Track To FIRST GRADE consists of weekly activity and game pages to send home to your families. We developed them because parents asked us how they could help their children learn at home. These weekly activity pages are tried and true! We have been successfully using them with the families in our classrooms for over five years.

The activities are developmentally appropriate to promote fine and gross motor, language, reading, and math readiness skills. Our young children and their families have come to call the sheets their "homework" so they can be like their older brothers and sisters.

Using the Weekly Activity Sheets

At the beginning of the year, send a note home to explain the purpose and format of the weekly activity sheets.

(A sample letter is included on the next page.)

Each Week

1. Duplicate the Weekly Activity Sheets and Game Pages.

2. Send the Sheets home to your families on Monday.

3. Have the children return the Activity Sheets on Friday.

4. Keep each child's work in a separate folder.

This:

- Keeps the Activity Sheets organized.

- Gives parents access to review and repeat the activities.

- Helps parents recognize their child's progress during the year.

5. Use the **MY SUMMER JOURNAL** sheets in July and August.

6. Use the BOOK LIST as a quick reference for great book selections.

We wish you success in using **On Track To FIRST GRADE!**

Alex and Barb

P.S. Remember this book with the Weekly Activity Sheets and Game Pages is also available in the Spanish edition of On Track To FIRST GRADE - Camino al PRIMER GRADO.

DEAR PARENTS

Let's work together this year to help your child learn reading, math, physical, and language readiness skills. Every Monday your child will bring home an Activity Sheet with five or more activities on it and Game Page. (Some children like to call these sheets their "Homework.")

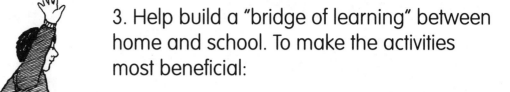

Each Activity Sheet has three main purposes. To:

1. Encourage fun and quality time with your child.

2. Help reinforce age-appropriate skills and concepts.

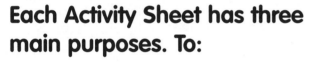

3. Help build a "bridge of learning" between home and school. To make the activities most beneficial:

- Find a quiet place and time to work.

- Take a few minutes to do the physical activities and exercises daily. The muscles need regular exercise to get stronger and more coordinated.

- Try to make reading to your child a part of your daily routine. The research shows that children who are read to on a regular basis have an easier time learning to read.

- Have your child color or put a small check in the corner of each activity to show that it has been finished.

Enjoy doing the activities with your child. Please return the sheet(s) to school every Friday.

HAVE FUN!

QUESTION OF THE WEEK

How do you get to school everyday?

_____

On Track To FIRST GRADE

September ~ Week 1

 Have someone read to you. *Who/what was the story about?*

Tell someone 5 things about yourself.

I like to run.

_____

Kick a ball around outside.

Play CONNECT THE DOTS

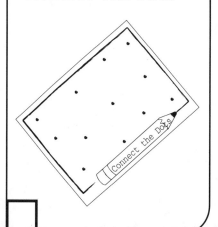

Connect the Dots

Draw and Color

a picture of yourself on a piece of paper.

It's me.

Child's Name _____   **Parent's Name** _____

www.bblocksonline.com

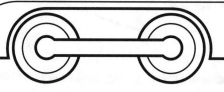
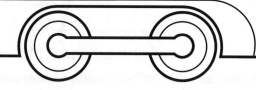

9

Connect the Dots

Connect the Dots - Connect the dots any way you want. Color the sections different colors.

On Track To FIRST GRADE

September ~ Week 3

Have someone read to you.

Who was your favorite character in the story? Why?

Tell 5 people when your birthday is.

March 8

Jump up and down, clap your hands and count to 10.

Can you do it again and count to 20?

1, 2, 3....

Try doing this everyday.

Draw and Color

a picture of your teacher on a paper plate.

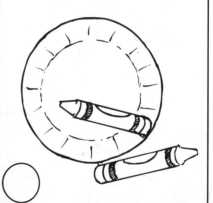

Look at SAMMY SHAPE. Name all his shapes.

Sammy Shape

Child's Name _____   **Parent's Name** _____

www.bblocksonline.com

13

Sammy Shape – Point to each of Sammy's shapes and call out what it is.

14

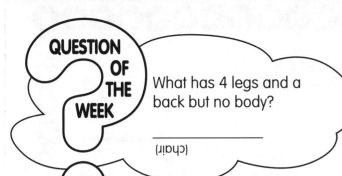

On Track To FIRST GRADE

September ~ Week 4

 Have someone read to you.

Where did the story take place?

How do you get ready for school? Tell someone what you do:

___ First

___ Next

___ Last

Play volleyball with a beach ball.

Go to the library. Did you check out any books?

___ Yes

___ No

Play HEADS OR TAILS.

 Sing Good Morning.

Child's Name _____ **Parent's Name** _____

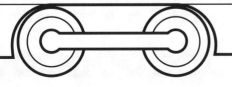

www.bblocksonline.com

15

Heads or Tails

Name: _____   Name: _____   Name: _____

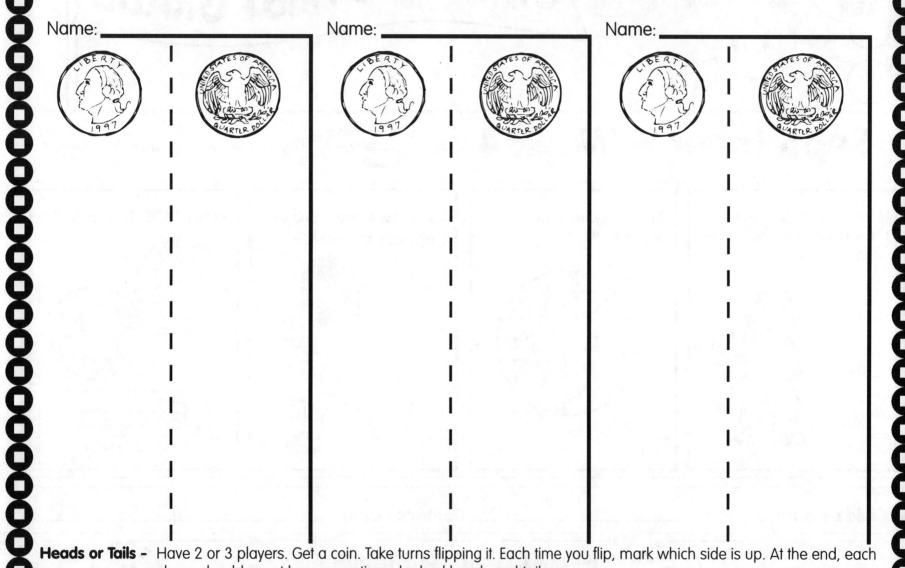

Heads or Tails – Have 2 or 3 players. Get a coin. Take turns flipping it. Each time you flip, mark which side is up. At the end, each player should count how many times he had heads and tails.

QUESTION OF THE WEEK

Do you have any loose teeth?

____ Yes ____ No

On Track To FIRST GRADE

October ~ Week 1

 Have someone read to you.

Name all the characters in the story.

How many times can you throw a ball up in the air and catch it?

_____

Sing the ABC SONG.
Point to the letters as you sing.

Draw and Color

a picture of your family on a large paper bag.

Ask Mom or Dad for some "junk mail." Circle and name all the numbers you can find.

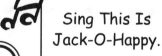 Sing This Is Jack-O-Happy.

Child's Name _____   **Parent's Name** _____

www.bblocksonline.com

17

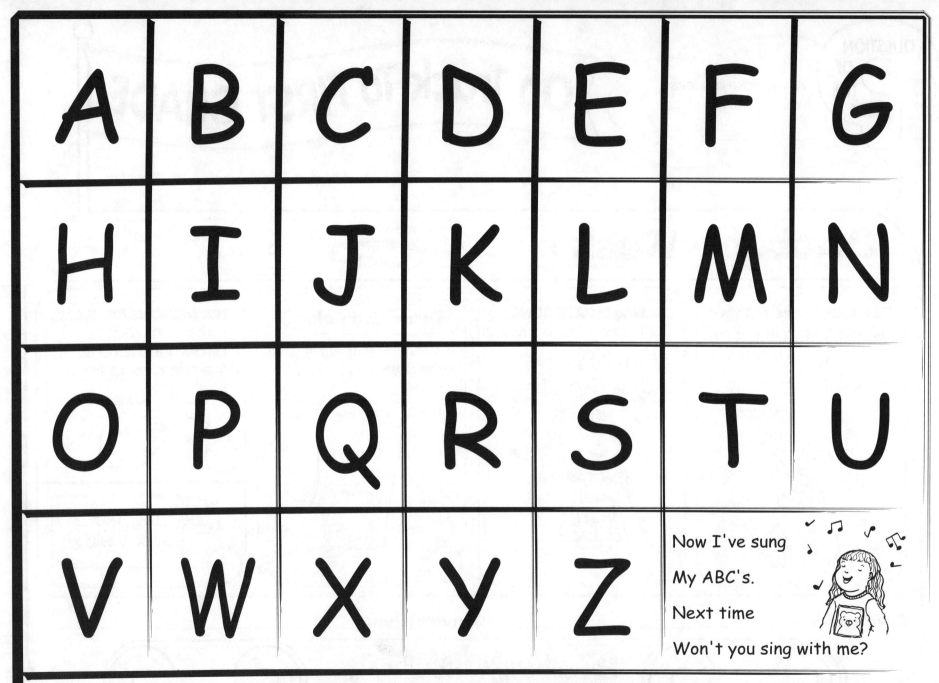

A	B	C	D	E	F	G
H	I	J	K	L	M	N
O	P	Q	R	S	T	U
V	W	X	Y	Z		

Now I've sung

My ABC's.

Next time

Won't you sing with me?

Point and Sing - Point to each letter as you sing the ABC SONG.

www.bblocksonline.com

Why does a firefighter wear red suspenders?

(to keep his pants up)

On Track To FIRST GRADE

October ~ Week 2

Have someone read to you.

Retell the story in your own words.

Practice a fire drill in your house.

Tell 5 people how to spell your name.

Dan

Practice STOP, DROP, and ROLL.

Clothes on fire? Don't get scared.
STOP!
DROP!
and ROLL!
by Dick Wilmes

Play catch with someone.

Draw and Color

a picture of where you live on a piece of paper.

Child's Name _____

Parent's Name _____

BUILDING BLOCKS

www.bblocksonline.com

19

Stop

Drop

Stop, Drop, and Roll
Clothes on fire?
Don't get scared.

STOP!
DROP! and
ROLL!
by Dick Wilmes

and Roll

STOP! DROP! and ROLL! - Pretend that your clothes are on fire. Do the STOP, DROP, and ROLL move. Practice it 3 times. Hang the poster on your refrigerator. Practice once a week.

QUESTION OF THE WEEK

What is your favorite kind of treat?

_____

On Track To FIRST GRADE

October ~ Week 3

Have someone read to you.

Was there a problem in the story? How did it get solved?

Go on a HAND HUNT.

Bigger than my hand

Smaller than my hand

☐

Say the days of the week everyday this week.

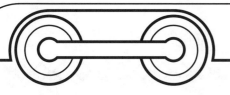

Monday...

Draw a long line on the sidewalk. Walk:

___ Forwards

___ Backwards

___ Sideways

___ Tip-toe

___ Toe-heel

Have Mom or Dad show you your street sign. Name each letter. What's the name of your street?

Oak Street

Draw and Color

3 jack-o-lanterns with 3 different faces on 3 paper plates.

Child's Name _____ Parent's Name _____

www.bblocksonline.com

21

Bigger than my hand

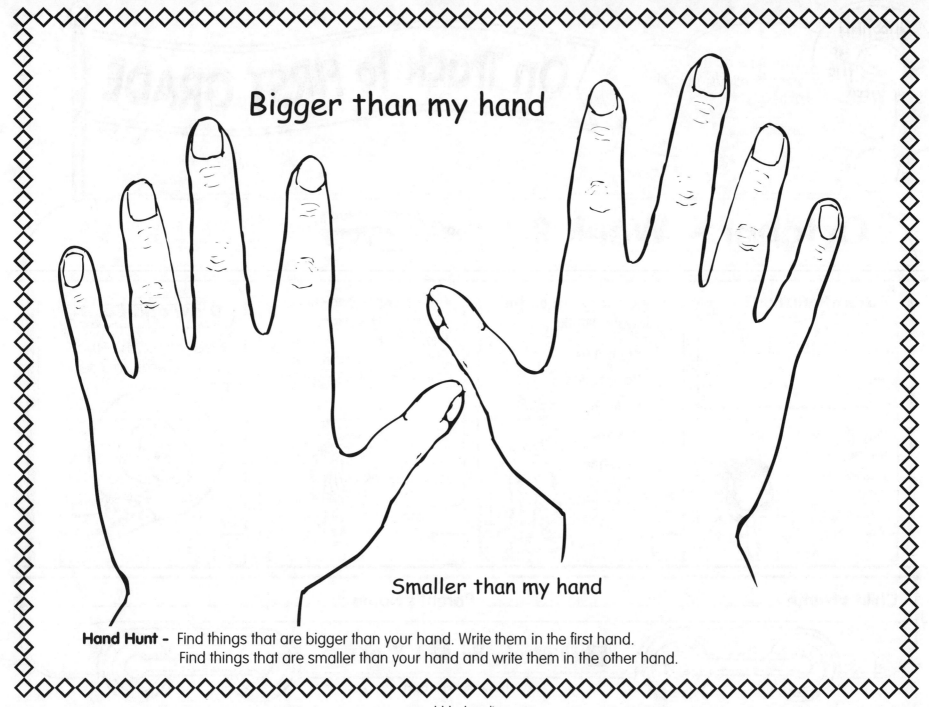

Smaller than my hand

Hand Hunt - Find things that are bigger than your hand. Write them in the first hand.
Find things that are smaller than your hand and write them in the other hand.

What is round and orange, and sometimes has a face?

_____
(pumpkin)

On Track To FIRST GRADE

October ~ Week 4

Have someone read to you.

What was your favorite picture? Why do you like it best?

Go for a walk and count pumpkins.

How many did you see?

◯ _____

Draw and Color

a picture of 10 pumpkins in a row on a long piece of paper.

Put the **CARVE YOUR PUMPKIN Puzzle** *together.*

◯

Play MEMORY
Have 8 - 10 pairs of playing cards turned upside down on the table. The first player turns 2 cards over, trying to make a match. If he does, he keeps them; if not, he turns them back over. Continue playing until all the cards are matched.

◯

Child's Name _____

Parent's Name _____

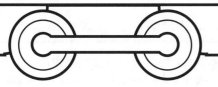  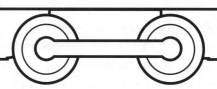

www.bblocksonline.com

23

Carve A Pumpkin _____

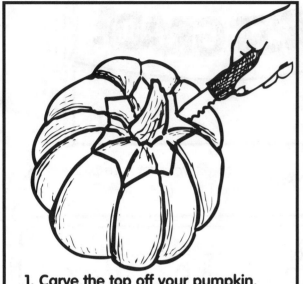

1. Carve the top off your pumpkin.

2. Scoop out the pumpkin seeds.

3. Draw a face on your pumpkin.

4. Carefully carve your pumpkin face.

5. Light your pumpkin.

6. Watch your pumpkin glow.

Carve A Pumpkin - Cut out the 6 pieces to the puzzle. Mix them up and put them back together in the right order.

www.bblocksonline.com

What kind of car do you have?

_____

On Track To FIRST GRADE

November ~ Week 1

Have someone read to you.

Find your favorite page in the story.

NAME
5 parts of a car.

Do:
_____ 5 sit-ups

_____ 5 push-ups

Can you do more?

____ Yes ____ No

How many?

_____

Sing
I'M A LITTLE TEAPOT.

WHAT'S THE WEATHER TODAY?

Chart the weather for 1 week.

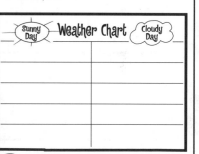

Child's Name _____   Parent's Name _____

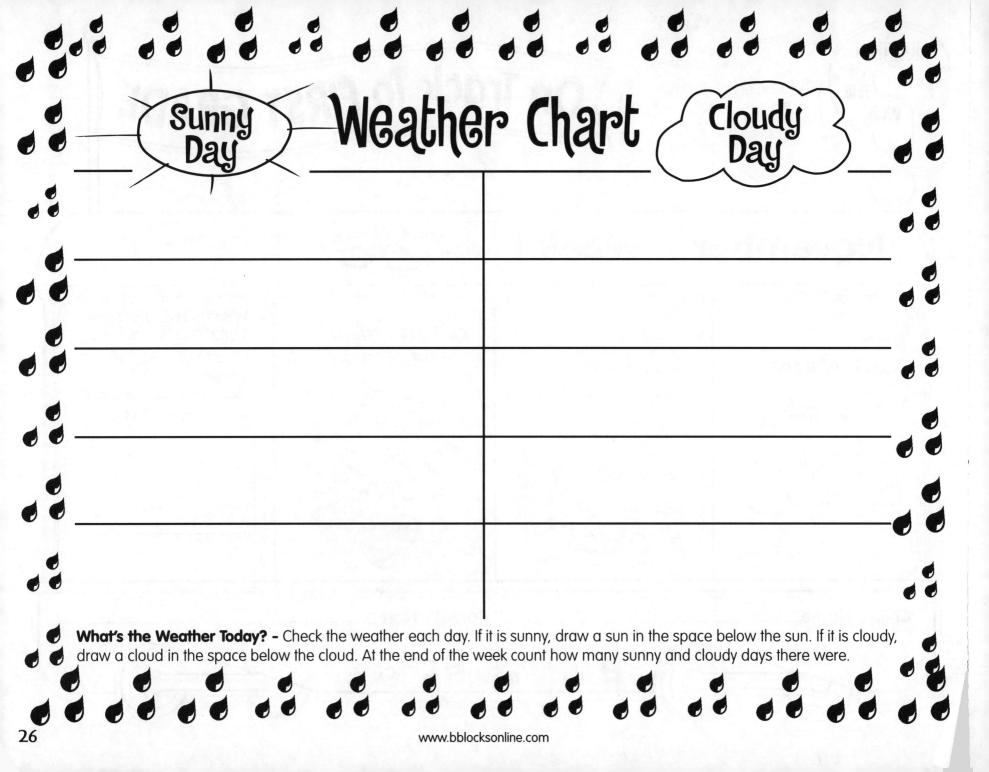

Weather Chart

Sunny Day

Cloudy Day

What's the Weather Today? - Check the weather each day. If it is sunny, draw a sun in the space below the sun. If it is cloudy, draw a cloud in the space below the cloud. At the end of the week count how many sunny and cloudy days there were.

On Track To FIRST GRADE

November ~ Week 2

 Have someone read to you.

Retell the story in your own words.

Play WHICH ONE DOESN'T BELONG?

Hat, chair, coat, mittens.

CRAB WALK
Do the crab walk from the living room to the kitchen.

Learn and recite **THE TURKEY IS A FUNNY BIRD.**

Gobble, gobble, gobble

Draw and Color
a turkey with lots of feathers. Trace around your hand and fingers to start.

Child's Name _____   **Parent's Name** _____

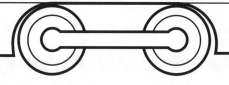  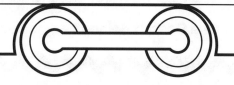

BUILDING BLOCKS

www.bblocksonline.com

Which One Doesn't Belong?

Ball Balloon Grass Frisbee	Hat Chair Coat Mittens	Hot Dog French Fries Tree Ice cream
Boat Car Train House	Book Hammer Saw Screwdriver	Make up more of your own.

Which One Doesn't Belong? - Read each set of words. Ask your child, "Which one doesn't belong?" After he answers, ask "Why?"

On Track To FIRST GRADE

November ~ Week 3

Have someone read to you.

Did you like the story? Why?

How many do you have:

___ Brothers?

___ Sisters?

___ Grandparents?

___ Aunts?

___ Uncles?

___ Cousins?

Stand on one foot and count to:

___ 5

___ 10

1, 2, 3, 4...

Try the other foot.

WRITE YOUR NAME.

How many times can you write your first name?

I can write my first name!

Name:

___ *4 fruits*

___ *4 vegetables*

Child's Name _____

Parent's Name _____

I can write my first name!

I Can Write My Name – Write your first name. Go back, point to each letter and name it.

On Track To FIRST GRADE

November ~ Week 4

 Have someone read to you. *What was the story about?*

Name 2-3 foods that are:

____ Salty

____ Sweet

____ Sour

Play TOUCH

You need 2 players. One player names 2 body parts such as *"finger to nose."* The second player touches his finger to his nose. Switch. The second player names 2 body parts, such as *"wrist to cheek."* and the first player touches his wrist to his cheek.

Continue naming body parts and touching.

Help set the table.

Do I AM THANKFUL.

I am Thankful

Name _____

♪ Sing We Eat Turkey.

Child's Name _____

Parent's Name _____

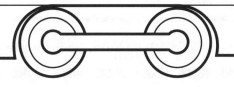

 BUILDING BLOCKS

www.bblocksonline.com

31

I am Thankful

_____
Name

I Am Thankful – Talk with your child about all the things and people he likes and is thankful for. Write them on the wishbone.

On Track To FIRST GRADE

December ~ Week 1

Have someone read to you.

Did you think anything was funny in the story? What?

WHAT'S MISSING?

Put 6-7 things in a row. Have your child close his eyes. Take one away. Open eyes and tell WHAT'S MISSING.

Mix up the objects and play again and again.

Hold a ball over your head and stand on one foot.

Count to:

___ 5

___ 10

Do the NUMBER PUZZLE.

HOLIDAY CHAIN

1. Cut 5-7, 2"x6" paper strips.
2. Have the players name things they would like to receive for holiday gifts.
3. Write each gift on a strip.
4. Staple the links together and hang the chain for the family to see.

Child's Name _____ **Parent's Name** _____

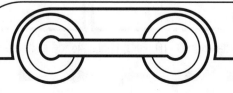

BUILDING BLOCKS

www.bblocksonline.com

33

Number Puzzle

0 1 2 3 4

5 6 7 8 9 10

Number Puzzle - Cut out the numbers. Mix them up and place them on a placemat or cookie sheet. Put them in order from 0 -10. For a challenge, do them backwards.

On Track To FIRST GRADE

December ~ Week 2

 Have someone read to you. *Retell the story.*

Tell someone 10 holiday words.
Who did you tell?

_____

candles
presents
cookies

What holiday(s) does your family celebrate?

___ Hanukkah?   ___ Christmas?
___ Kwanzaa?   _____ (other)   Kwanzaa

Tell your Mom or Dad what your favorite thing is about the holiday(s).

Hop up and down on one foot.

Hop up and down on the other foot.

Keep practicing.

♫ Sing
THE MORE
WE GET
TOGETHER.

**Play
NUMBER COVER-UP.**

Number Cover-Up			
1	2	11	12
3	4	13	14
5	6	15	16
7	8	17	18
9	10	19	20

Child's Name _____   **Parent's Name** _____

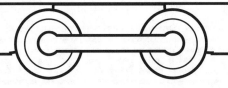

Number Cover-Up

1	**2**	**11**	**12**
3	**4**	**13**	**14**
5	**6**	**15**	**16**
7	**8**	**17**	**18**
9	**10**	**19**	**20**

Number Cover-Up - Get a bottle cap. First play with the 1-10 card. Call out a number and have your child cover it up. Call out another number and have him move his bottle cap to cover that number. Continue until he's covered each number at least once. On another day, play **Number Cover-Up** with the 11 - 20 card.

QUESTION OF THE WEEK

What comes in any shape, is wrapped in paper, and is fun to open?

_____
(present)

On Track To FIRST GRADE

December ~ Week 3

Have someone read to you.

Were there any animals in the story? If so name them.

Find and circle these letters, B - S - R - T, in a newspaper or magazine.

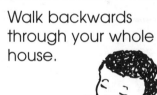

Walk backwards through your whole house.

Make CORNSTARCH GOOP.

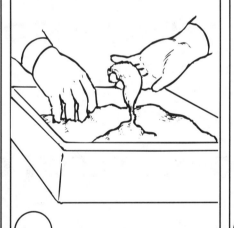

Find someone who weighs:

___ **More than you**

___ **Less than you**

Child's Name _____   **Parent's Name** _____

www.bblocksonline.com

37

CORN STARCH GOOP

Supplies

11/2 cups of corn starch

1/2 cup water

Food coloring (optional)

Large shallow pan such as a brownie pan

Make CORN STARCH GOOP

1. Pour the cornstarch in a bowl.

2. (Optional) Add the food coloring to your water.

3. Slowly add the water, mixing with a spoon or your fingers.

Play With CORN STARCH GOOP

Pour the CORNSTARCH GOOP in the brownie pan. Poke, push, and spread the dough for as long as you want.

Children love this dough. It feels so good in their hands and is very soothing. It also changes as they play with it. The dough literally melts in their hands when they touch it, and then becomes firmer when they leave it alone.

CORNSTARCH STARCH GOOP – Make CORN STARCH GOOP. It is so soothing to touch.

On Track To FIRST GRADE

December ~ Week 4

 Have someone read to you.

See if you can remember all the characters in your story.

Go on a WINTER SCAVENGER HUNT.

Play CHARADES

One player pretends to play one of the sports. Everyone else guesses what sport it is. Take turns. For example:

___ Golf
___ Baseball
___ Swimming
___ Tennis
___ Basketball
___ Soccer
___ Football
___ Bowling

Play STORE using some of your toys.

Play HOT and COLD

Have a player hide a toy.

Start looking for the toy. As you get closer to the toy, the first player calls out, "hot." If you go farther away, the player calls out, "cold." Continue until you've found the toy.

Child's Name _____   **Parent's Name** _____

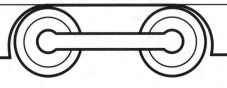  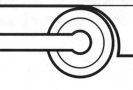

BUILDING BLOCKS

www.bblocksonline.com

39

Winter Scavenger Hunt

__ snowman

__ squirrel

__ snow shovel

__ bird

__ child dressed for winter

__ sled

__ tree

Outside Winter Scavenger Hunt - If you have snow in your area, take a walk. Check off each thing you see.

Inside Winter Scavenger Hunt - If you don't have snow, get out several magazines. Look for pictures of winter activity. Check off each thing you see.

What is your favorite sport?

_____

On Track To FIRST GRADE

January ~ Week 1

Have someone read to you.

What clothes did the characters wear?

Name 4 things that are:

_____ Hot _____ Cold

_____ Big _____ Little

_____ Hard _____ Soft

_____ Fast _____ Slow

Draw lots of straight lines using a ruler and pencil.

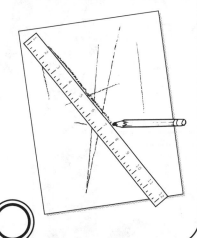

Tell 5 people what year it is.

HAPPY NEW YEAR

Sing
Twinkle Twinkle
Little Star.

EXERCISE TIME

Hang the poster.
Exercise everyday.

Child's Name _____   **Parent's Name** _____

www.bblocksonline.com

41

EXERCISE TIME

Jump

Jumping Jack

Fly

Skate

March

Crawl

Wiggle

Tiptoe

What falls from the sky, and is white and cold?

_____

(Snowflake)

On Track To FIRST GRADE

January ~ Week 2

 Have someone read to you.

Retell the story in your own words.

Do the ALPHABET PUZZLE.

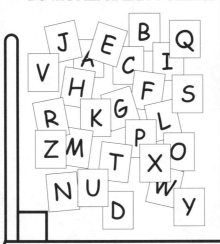

SNOWBALL TOSS

Crumple 1/2 sheets of newspaper to make snowballs. Toss them into an empty box or large paper bag.

STORY TIME

Make up a story about a penguin and a polar bear. Tell it to your mom or dad.

Say the months of the year. Try saying them everyday this week.

January, February, March, April, May....

Child's Name _____   **Parent's Name** _____

 BUILDING BLOCKS

ALPHABET PUZZLE

A B C D E
F G H I J K L
M N O P Q R S
T U V W X Y Z

ALPHABET PUZZLE — Cut out the letters. Mix them up and put them on a cookie sheet. Put the alphabet together in order. Keep the letters in an envelope. Put the **ALPHABET PUZZLE** together another day.

On Track To FIRST GRADE

January ~ Week 3

Have someone read to you.

What was your favorite part of the story?
Retell that part to someone.

NURSERY RHYME FUN
Have someone read the rhymes to you, stopping every couple of words for you to fill in the next word.

Have fun exercising. Do these 10 times each:

_____ Bend and touch your toes

_____ Do jumping jacks

_____ Jog in place

Have an ice cube melting race. Each player put his ice cube on a plate. "Go." Watch the ice cubes. Which one melted first? Last?

Find and Count
the hats in your house. How *many* did you find?

———————————

Child's Name _____   **Parent's Name** _____

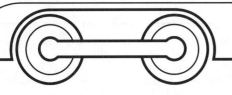  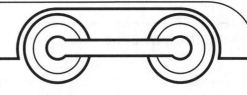

www.bblocksonline.com

45

JACK AND JILL

Jack and _____ went
(Jill)

Up the _____,
(hill)

To fetch a pail of _____.
(water)

Jack fell _____ and
(down)

Broke his _____.
(crown)

And _____ came
(Jill)

Tumbling _____.
(after)

HICKORY, DICKORY, DOC

Hickory, Dickory, _____.
(Doc)

The _____ ran up
(mouse)

The _____.
(clock)

The clock struck _____.
(one)

The _____ ran down.
(mouse)

Hickory, _____, Doc.
(Dickory)

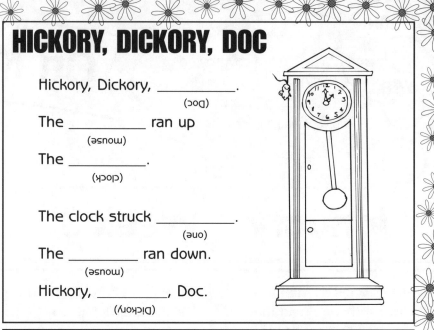

LITTLE MISS MUFFET

Little Miss _____
(Muffet)

Sat on a _____
(tuffet)

Eating her curds and _____.
(whey)

Along came a _____
(spider)

And sat down _____
(beside her)

And _____
(frightened)

Miss _____ away.
(Muffet)

HUMPTY DUMPTY

Humpty _____ sat
(Dumpty)

On a _____.
(wall)

Humpty _____ had
(Dumpty)

A great _____.
(fall)

All the king's _____
(horses)

And all the king's _____
(men)

Couldn't put _____
(Humpty)

Together _____.
(again)

NURSERY RHYME FUN — Read these nursery rhymes to your child, stopping every couple of words for him to fill in the next word.

On Track To FIRST GRADE

January ~ Week 4

Have someone read to you.

After the story ask, _"If you could be a character in the story, who would you be? Why?"_

Put an unbreakable cup filled 3/4 full of water in the freezer. Take it out tomorrow and tell what happened. Set it in the sink. Keep watching it.

What is happening?

Play **LINKING LETTERS.**

I can LINK MY LETTERS!
ABCDEFGHIJKLMNOPQRSTUVWXYZ

hat
bat
cat

RHYME TIME
List words that rhyme with "hat," "dot" and "pan."

Play **SQUARE UP.**

Child's Name _____

Parent's Name _____

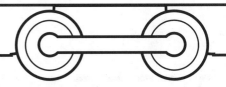  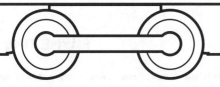

BUILDING BLOCKS

www.bblocksonline.com

47

Rhyme Time

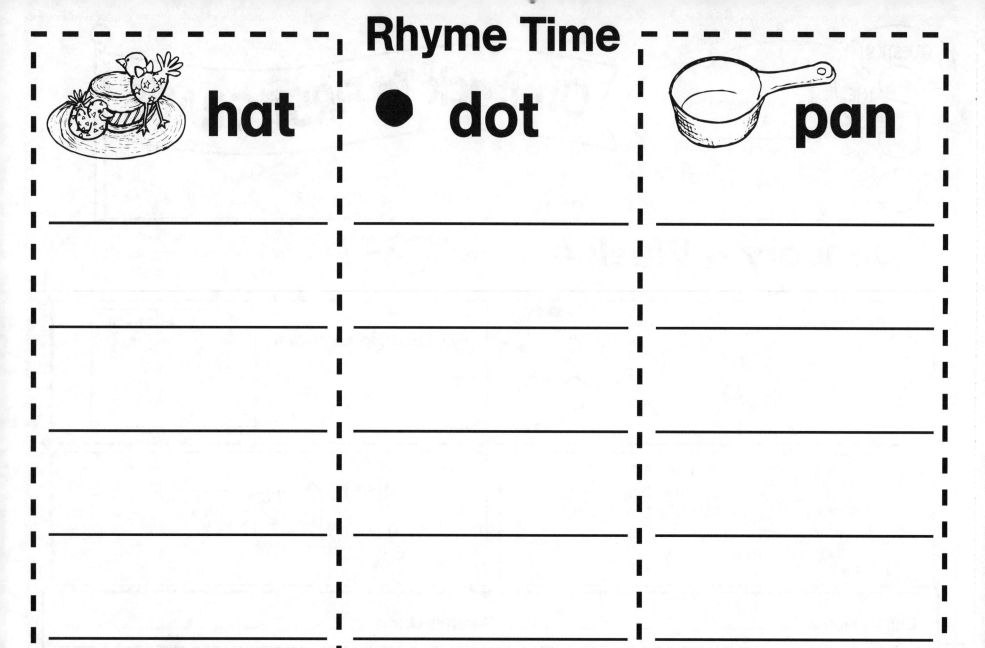

hat

● dot

pan

RHYME TIME — Say the word at the top. List words that rhyme with it.

Square Up

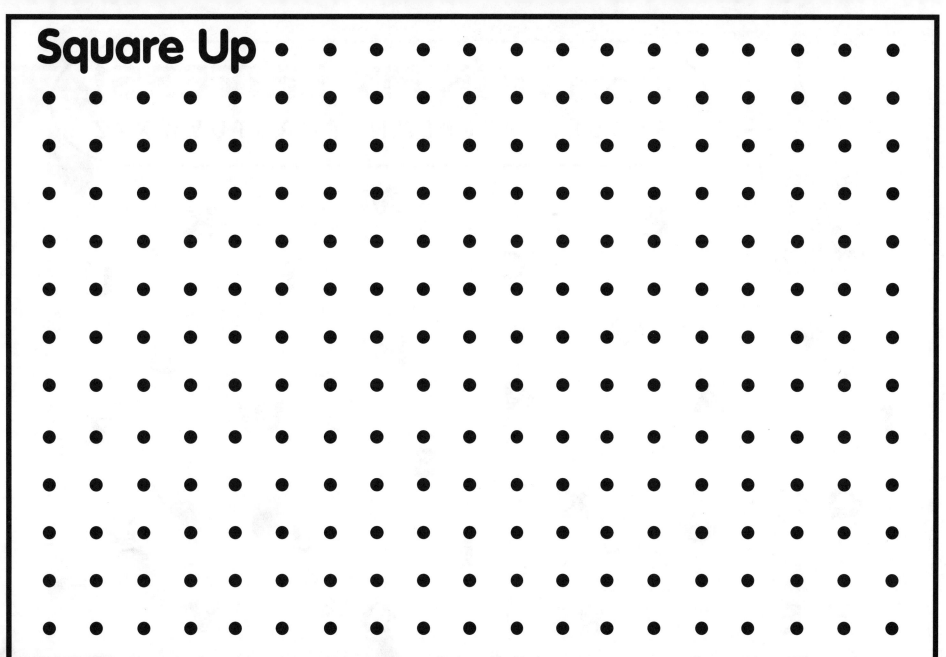

SQUARE UP — Have the first player draw a line connecting 2 dots. Each player in turn connects 2 more dots. When a player connects 2 dots which make a square, he should put his initial in it. Continue playing until all the dots are connected. Let each player count how many squares he made.

I can **LINK MY LETTERS!**

ABCDEFGHIJKLMNOPQRSTUVWXYZ

LINKING LETTERS — Starting with "A," link all the letters together in the right order. If you want, connect them again and again, each time with a different color. Count how many times you linked the letters together.

Where do your grandparents live?

_____

On Track To FIRST GRADE

February ~ Week 1

Have someone read to you.

Where did the story take place? Describe it.

ME AND MY SHADOW

Hang the poster and copy the shadows.

Turn on music and dance.

Can you dance to one more song?

____ Yes

____ No

Draw and Color

lots of hearts on white paper. Color them different colors.

Sing IF YOU'RE HAPPY AND YOU KNOW IT.

COUNT how many steps you take to walk from your kitchen to your:

____ Bedroom ____ Bathroom

____ Living room

1, 2, 3...

Child's Name _____

Parent's Name _____

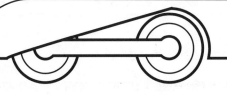

BUILDING BLOCKS

www.bblocksonline.com

51

ME and MY SHADOW

ME AND MY SHADOW — Tape the Shadow Poster to the mirror. Copy each shadow.

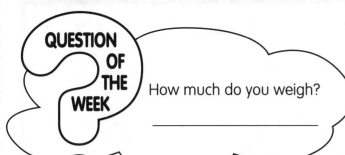

QUESTION OF THE WEEK

How much do you weigh?

_____

On Track To FIRST GRADE

February ~ Week 2

Have someone read to you. *Retell the story in your own words.*

Tell someone what makes you feel:

_____ Happy

_____ Sad

_____ Angry

_____ Afraid

I'm happy when I dance.

Make an airplane with your body and hold it for 10 seconds?

Make an egg with your body and hold it for 10 seconds?

Draw and Color

a picture of you and your best friend playing together.

After you're finished, show someone your picture and tell them what you and your friend are playing.

Talk about **LOVE BUG**.

"Love Bug" Shows Lots of **LOVE**

Sing 1 LITTLE, 2 LITTLE, 3 LITTLE HEARTS.

Child's Name _____

Parent's Name _____

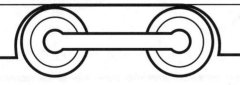  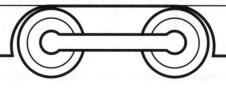

BUILDING BLOCKS

www.bblocksonline.com

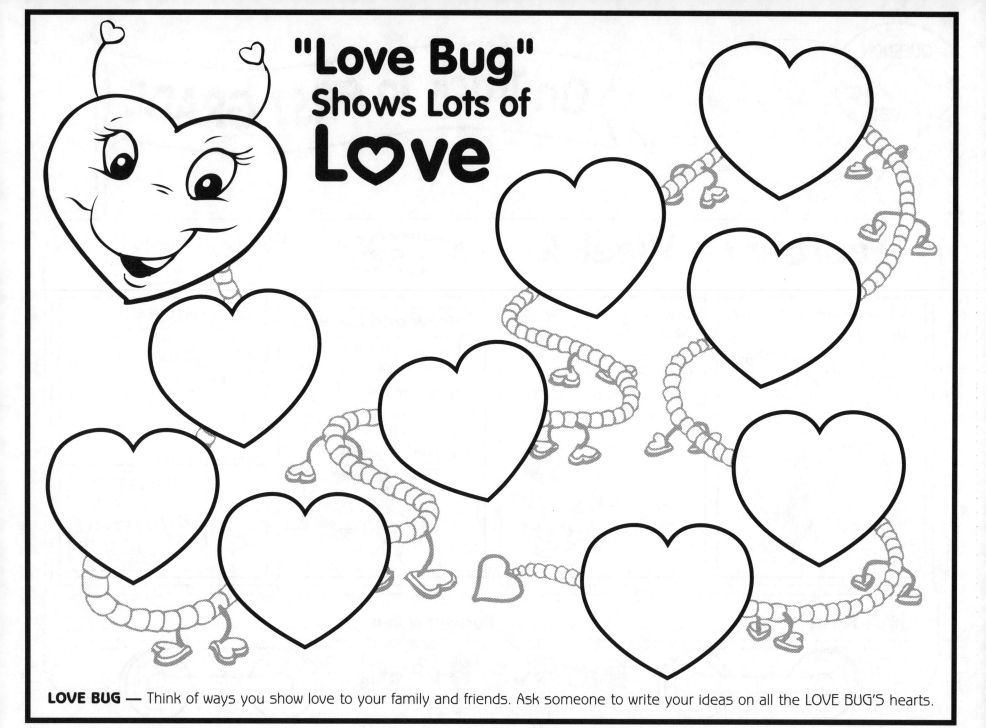

"Love Bug"
Shows Lots of
Love

LOVE BUG — Think of ways you show love to your family and friends. Ask someone to write your ideas on all the LOVE BUG'S hearts.

On Track To FIRST GRADE

February ~ Week 3

Get 10 plastic bottle caps. Write 1-10 on them with black marker. Put them in a container.

Close your eyes and pick one. Open your eyes and read the number to your mom or dad. Keep playing.

Make a bridge with your body and hold it for 10 seconds?

Make a tunnel with your body and hold it for 10 seconds?

FUN DOUGH

Make FUN DOUGH with your mom or dad or use clay.

What shapes, letters, and numbers can you make? Can you make your name?

_____ Yes

_____ No

"WAR"

Play "WAR" with a deck of cards.

Child's Name _____ **Parent's Name** _____

BUILDING BLOCKS

www.bblocksonline.com

55

NO-COOK FUN DOUGH

Supplies

2 cups flour

2 Tablespoons salt

2 Tablespoons vegetable oil

2 teaspoons alum (See spice shelf.)

1 cup very hot water (Remember safety.)

Food coloring (optional)

Make FUN DOUGH

1. Mix the flour, salt, vegetable oil, and alum in a large bowl.

2. Add the food coloring to the water. (optional)

3. Pour the colored water into the mixture in the large bowl. Stir.

4. Once the FUN DOUGH is mixed and cool to the touch, put it on the table. Knead it until it is totally mixed.

Play With FUN DOUGH

Put the DOUGH on a tray or cookie sheet along with children's scissors and small containers.

Store FUN DOUGH

Keep the DOUGH in an airtight container. This dough does not last as long as cooked doughs. If it begins to dry out, add a little water and knead again.

February ~ Week 4

 Have someone read to you. *Talk about the illustrations.*

Sing JOHNNY WORKS WITH ONE HAMMER.

Have someone hide a toy such as a teddy bear. Have the person give you hints until you have found it.

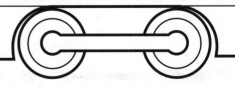

Play GREATER THAN — LESS THAN.

Toss a pair of dice and count the dots on each one. Tell someone which is "greater than" and which is "less than."

WRITE your first and last name.

Diana Dubois

Have a winter picnic indoors.

Child's Name _____

Parent's Name _____

www.bblocksonline.com

57

I can write my first and last name.

WRITE YOUR NAME — Write your whole name.

QUESTION OF THE WEEK

Are you right or left handed?

_____

On Track To FIRST GRADE

March ~ Week 1

Have someone read to you.

Have someone read a Dr. Seuss book to you. *What was the story about?*

I CAN RHYME

List words that rhyme with "dad," " bug" and "cold".

bug,
rug,
hug...

Put a 3 foot length of yarn or string on the floor.

Jump from side to side:

_____
10 times?

_____
15 times?

Play your favorite card game under a table.

Draw and Color

a picture of your favorite Dr. Seuss character on a paper plate.

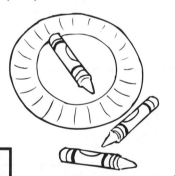

Child's Name _____   **Parent's Name** _____

BUILDING BLOCKS

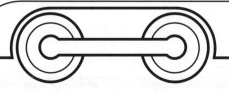 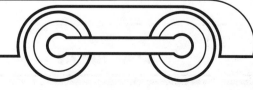

www.bblocksonline.com

59

I Can Rhyme

 dad  bug  cold

I CAN RHYME — Say the word at the top of each column. List words that rhyme with it.

What has a tail, a string, and flies on a windy day?

_____

(kite)

On Track To FIRST GRADE

March ~ Week 2

Have someone read to you.

Retell the story in your own words.

PUT THE alphabet puzzle TOGETHER.

alphabet puzzle	a	b	c	d	e
f	g	h	i	j	k	l
m	n	o	p	q	r	s
t	u	v	w	x	y	z

SILLY WORD

Make up a silly word. Write it down and draw a picture of what you think it looks like.

pickoslam

Play WHEELBARROW

Pick a partner and play on a carpeted area.

peanut butter, jelly

GO - TOGETHERS

Name 5 things that go together. Have someone write them down.

Child's Name _____

Parent's Name _____

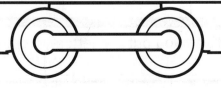

BUILDING BLOCKS

alphabet puzzle

a	b	c	d	e
f	g	h	i	j	k	l
m	n	o	p	q	r	s
t	u	v	w	x	y	z

alphabet puzzle — Cut out the letters. Put them on a cookie sheet. Sing the ABC SONG as you put the letters in order. Keep them in an envelop to play again.

My Silly Word

My silly word is_____

_____

MY SILLY WORD — Think of a silly word. Write it down. Draw a picture of what you think your silly word looks like.

Go-Togethers

Mystery Words

GO-TOGETHERS — Think of things that go together, like a bat and a ball. Write the pairs on the lines.

What is your favorite color?

_____

On Track To FIRST GRADE

March ~ Week 3

Have someone read to you.

Turn the pages for the person who is reading.

Name 4 of each:

_____ Animals

_____ Vehicles

_____ Stores

_____ Clothing

_____ Sports

Hop on 1 foot around the house.

Draw and Color

a rainbow on any type of paper you want.

 Sing ARE YOU SLEEPING?

MY PHONE NUMBER
Have Mom or Dad write your phone number.

Practice saying it.

847-742-10XX

Child's Name _____

Parent's Name _____

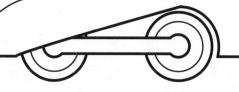

BUILDING BLOCKS

www.bblocksonline.com

My Phone Number

( )

_____

MY PHONE NUMBER — Write your phone number. Practice saying it.

www.bblocksonline.com

QUESTION OF THE WEEK

What do you get when you put 3 ducks in a box?

_____

(box of quackers)

March ~ Week 4

Have someone read to you.

Was there any part of the story you would like to change? What?

Name the opposite of:

_____ Hot
_____ Boy
_____ Up
_____ Happy
_____ Fast
_____ Big
_____ On
_____ In
_____ Top
_____ Wet

☐

Play FOLLOW THE LEADER. Be sure to:

____ March ____ Jump

____ Hop ____ Crawl

____ Gallop ____ Tip-toe

____ Run in place

☐

Help put the groceries away.

☐

Play TIC-TAC-TOE.

Play with different partners.

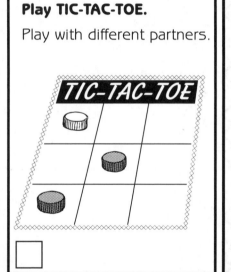

TIC-TAC-TOE

☐

Child's Name _____

Parent's Name _____

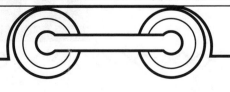

BUILDING BLOCKS

www.bblocksonline.com

67

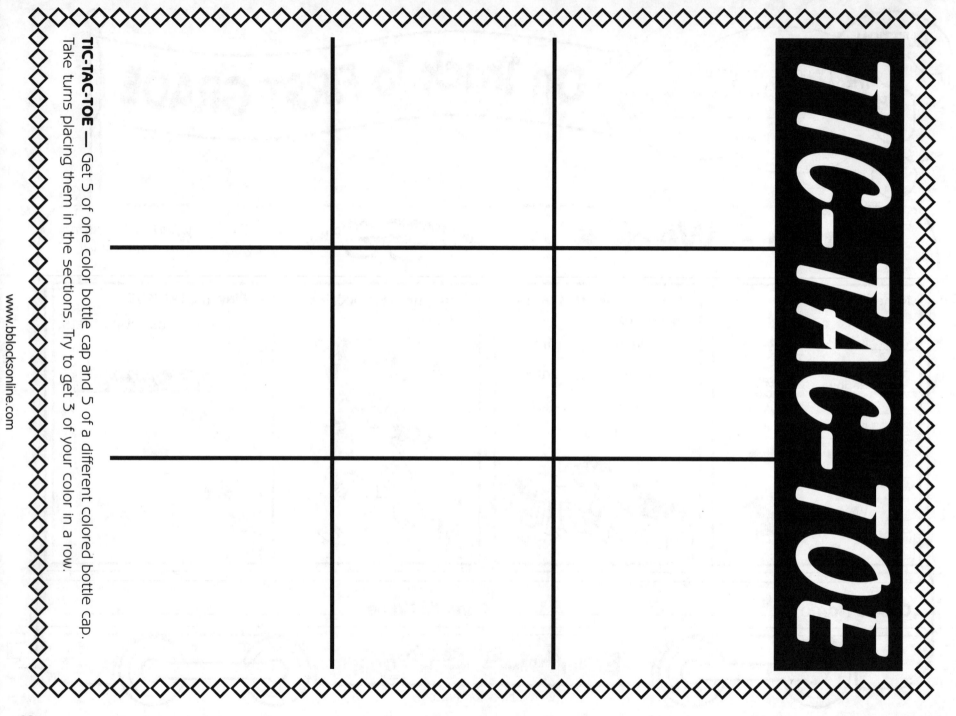

TIC-TAC-TOE — Get 5 of one color bottle cap and 5 of a different colored bottle cap. Take turns placing them in the sections. Try to get 3 of your color in a row.

TIC-TAC-TOE

www.bblocksonline.com

847-742-10XX

I can write my phone number.

CALL A FRIEND — Write your telephone number. Practice saying it and then tell it to 5 people. Call a friend.

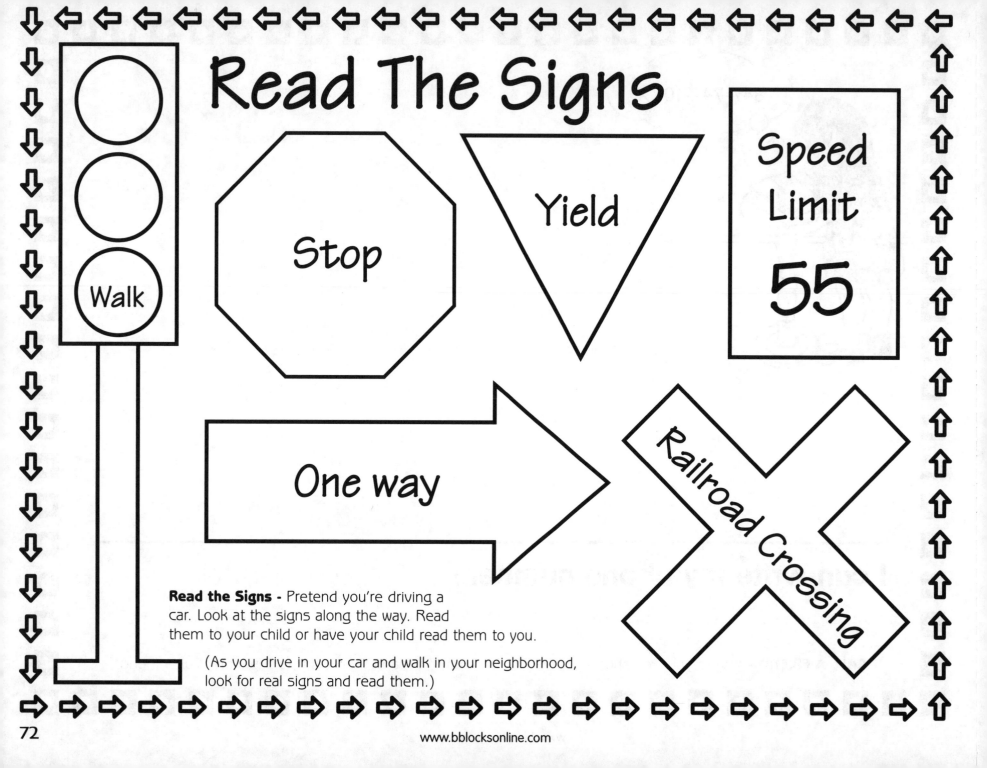

Read The Signs

Walk

Stop

Yield

Speed Limit 55

One way

Railroad Crossing

Read the Signs - Pretend you're driving a car. Look at the signs along the way. Read them to your child or have your child read them to you.

(As you drive in your car and walk in your neighborhood, look for real signs and read them.)

QUESTION OF THE WEEK

What is your favorite beverage?

_____

On Track To FIRST GRADE

April ~ Week 2

Have someone read to you.

Retell the story in your own words.

Name 5

__ Animals that can't fly.

__ Toys you like to play with.

__ Foods that you don't like.

Dribble
a ball down your sidewalk.

Make 5 different faces in the mirror.

Play **WHAT NUMBER AM I THINKING OF?**

Child's Name _____

Parent's Name _____

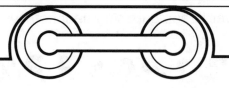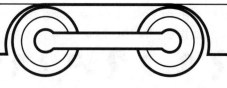

www.bblocksonline.com

73

What Number Am I Thinking Of?

Player 1

Player 2

WHAT NUMBER AM I THINKING OF? — Pick a range of numbers, such as 1-5 or 1-10. The first player thinks of a number, writes it in one of the boxes, and covers it up. The second player guesses.

The first player tells the second player to guess *"higher"* or *"lower."* The second player keeps guessing until he says the number written in the box. Switch and play again.

What goes up when the rain comes down?

_____

(umbrella)

On Track To FIRST GRADE

April ~ Week 3

Have someone read to you.

Does this story remind you of any other story you've ever read? Which one? Why?

Listen to or watch a weather report. Tell someone about the forecast.

Visit *a playground and play.* Did you play on the:

____ Swings?   ____ Slide?

____ Monkey bars?

Draw and Color

a picture of today's weather on a paper plate.

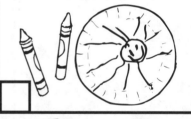

Chant 5 LITTLE MONKEYS

Put the

BABY BIRDS ARE BORN Puzzle together.

Baby Birds Are Born

The eggs are in the nest. | Mother Bird sits on the eggs.
The baby birds begin to hatch. | The baby birds are born.

Child's Name _____

Parent's Name _____

Baby Birds Are Born

The eggs are in the nest.

Mother Bird sits on the eggs.

The baby birds begin to hatch.

The baby birds are born.

BABY BIRDS ARE BORN Puzzle — Cut out the 4 pieces of the BABY BIRDS ARE BORN puzzle. Mix up the pieces and put the puzzle together. Save the pieces in an envelope. Put the puzzle together again.

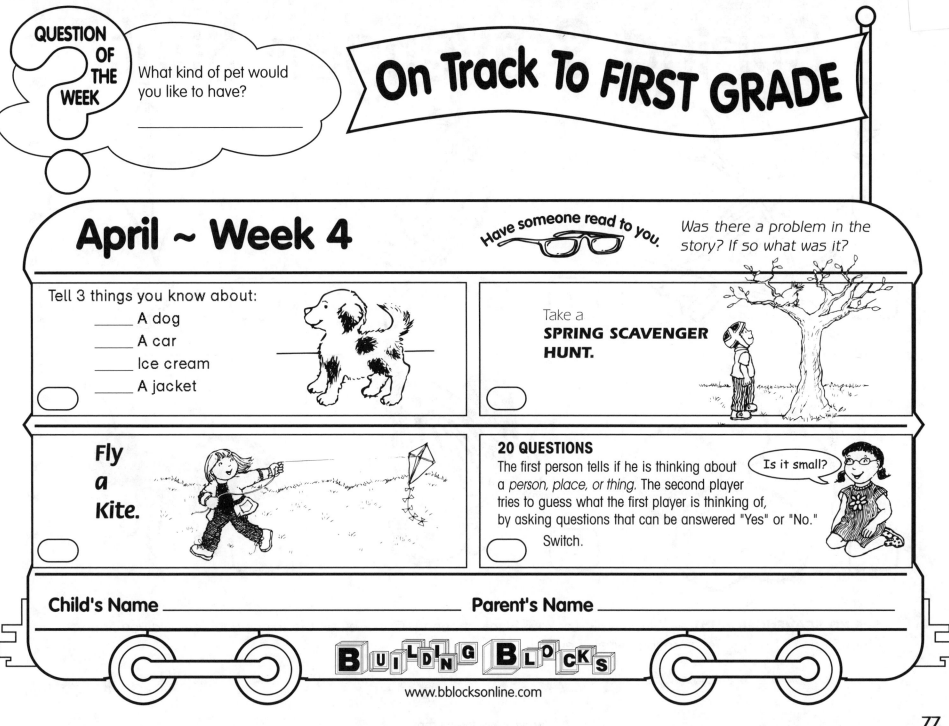

QUESTION OF THE WEEK

What kind of pet would you like to have?

_____

April ~ Week 4

Have someone read to you.

Was there a problem in the story? If so what was it?

Tell 3 things you know about:

_____ A dog
_____ A car
_____ Ice cream
_____ A jacket

Take a
SPRING SCAVENGER HUNT.

Fly a Kite.

20 QUESTIONS
The first person tells if he is thinking about a *person, place, or thing.* The second player tries to guess what the first player is thinking of, by asking questions that can be answered "Yes" or "No."

Switch.

Is it small?

Child's Name _____

Parent's Name _____

BUILDING BLOCKS

Spring Scavenger Hunt

SPRING SCAVENGER HUNT — Take a walk. Look for Signs of Spring. Check off all the things you see. Did you find other Signs of Spring? Tell someone what they are.

www.bblocksonline.com

QUESTION OF THE WEEK

What is your Mom's name? _____

On Track To FIRST GRADE

May ~ Week 1

 *Have someone read to you.* *Retell how the story ended.*

SINK AND FLOAT

Find 4 things that float and 4 things that sink.

Try them out in the sink.

Play JUMP!

Get a rope. Have 2 players hold the ends of the rope and slowly sway it back and forth.

The third player stands in the middle, facing one end. She jumps over the rope each time it comes close to the ground.

Take turns.

Sing THE FARMER PLANTS THE SEEDS.

The farmer plants....

Draw and Color

a picture of your Mom on a piece of paper you think she would like.

Mom

Child's Name _____

Parent's Name _____

BUILDING BLOCKS

www.bblocksonline.com

79

Sink

Float

SINK AND FLOAT — Find 4 things that sink and 4 things that float. Try them in your sink. Have someone help you write them.

QUESTION OF THE WEEK

What size shoe do you wear?

_____

On Track To FIRST GRADE

May ~ Week 2

Have someone read to you. _Retell the story in your own words._

FIND AND READ

5 signs to someone. Who did you read them to?

_____

Have different RACES:

____ Run a race.

____ Skip a race.

____ Crawl a race.

____ Hop a race.

Play **CONNECT THE NUMBERS.**

Twinkle, twinkle...

Go outside and look at the stars. Do you see any shapes or animals?

Child's Name _____ **Parent's Name** _____

www.bblocksonline.com

81

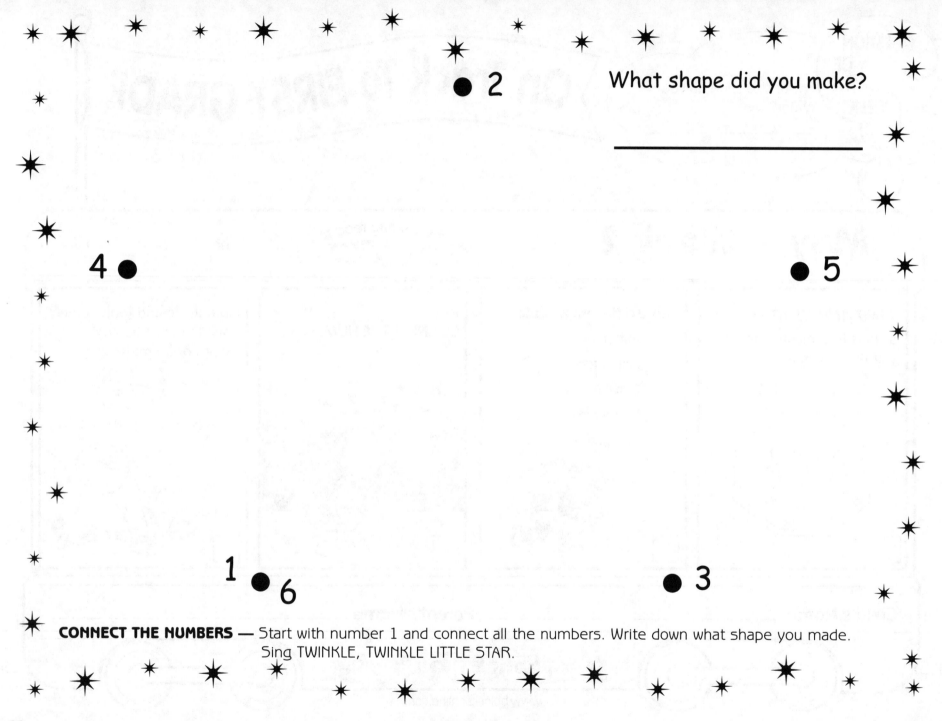

● 2

What shape did you make?

_____

4 ●

● 5

1 ● 6

● 3

CONNECT THE NUMBERS — Start with number 1 and connect all the numbers. Write down what shape you made.
Sing TWINKLE, TWINKLE LITTLE STAR.

On Track To FIRST GRADE

May ~ Week 3

Have someone read to you.

Pick your favorite character. Count how many times he/she is pictured in the story.

Trace a shadow on the sidewalk with chalk.

POP THE BUBBLES

Have someone blow bubbles in the air. Pop as many as you can with your elbows.

Play again and again, each time popping them with a different body part.

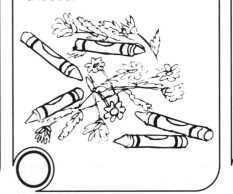

Draw and Color

a picture of spring flowers on any piece of paper you choose.

MY ADDRESS

Write your address.

Practice it and then tell 5 people your address.

16 OAK

Child's Name _____   **Parent's Name** _____

BUILDING BLOCKS

www.bblocksonline.com

My Address is

MY ADDRESS — Write your address.

What sport do you play?

_____

On Track To FIRST GRADE

May ~ Week 4

Have someone read to you. Stop before you finish reading. Ask *"How do you think the story will end"*? Continue reading. Talk about how it really ended.

Name 5 parts of a bicycle:

1. _____
2. _____
3. _____
4. _____
5. _____

SHAPE-UP - Follow the dashes. Show someone what shapes you made.

SHAPE-UP

circle

rectangle

square

oval

triangle

Make SIDEWALK CHALK. Write your name on the sidewalk. How many times did you write it?

_____

Go for a LISTENING WALK.

CROSSING GUARD

PLAY I SPY.

The first player sees something, such as a "ladybug." He gives the second player clues about it. The second player keeps listening to the clues and guessing what it could be.

Switch.

Child's Name _____   **Parent's Name** _____

BUILDING BLOCKS

www.bblocksonline.com

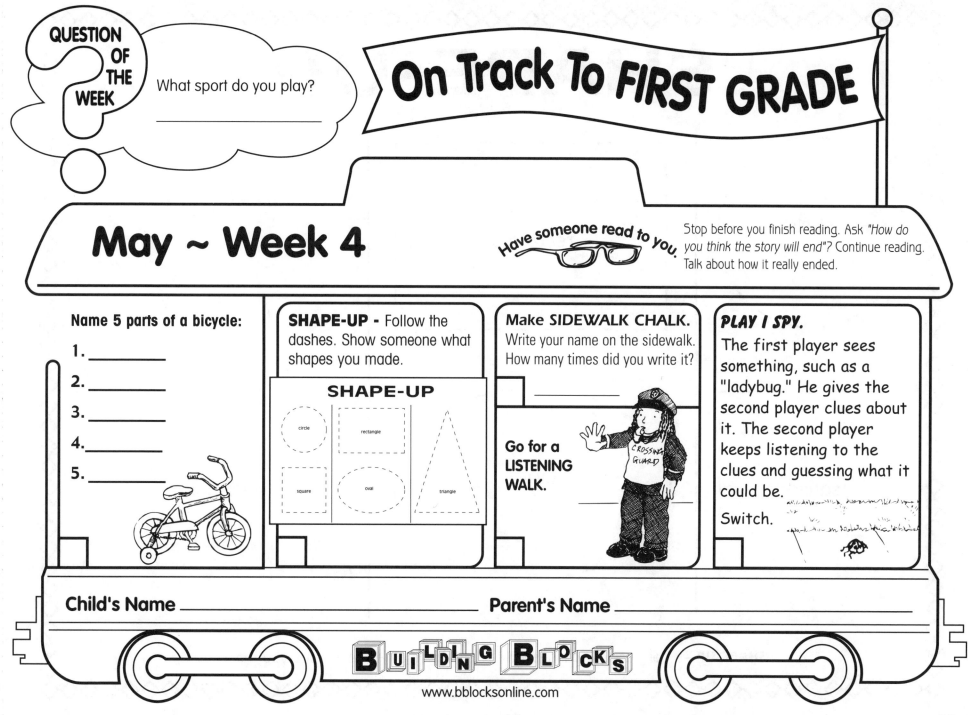

SHAPE-UP

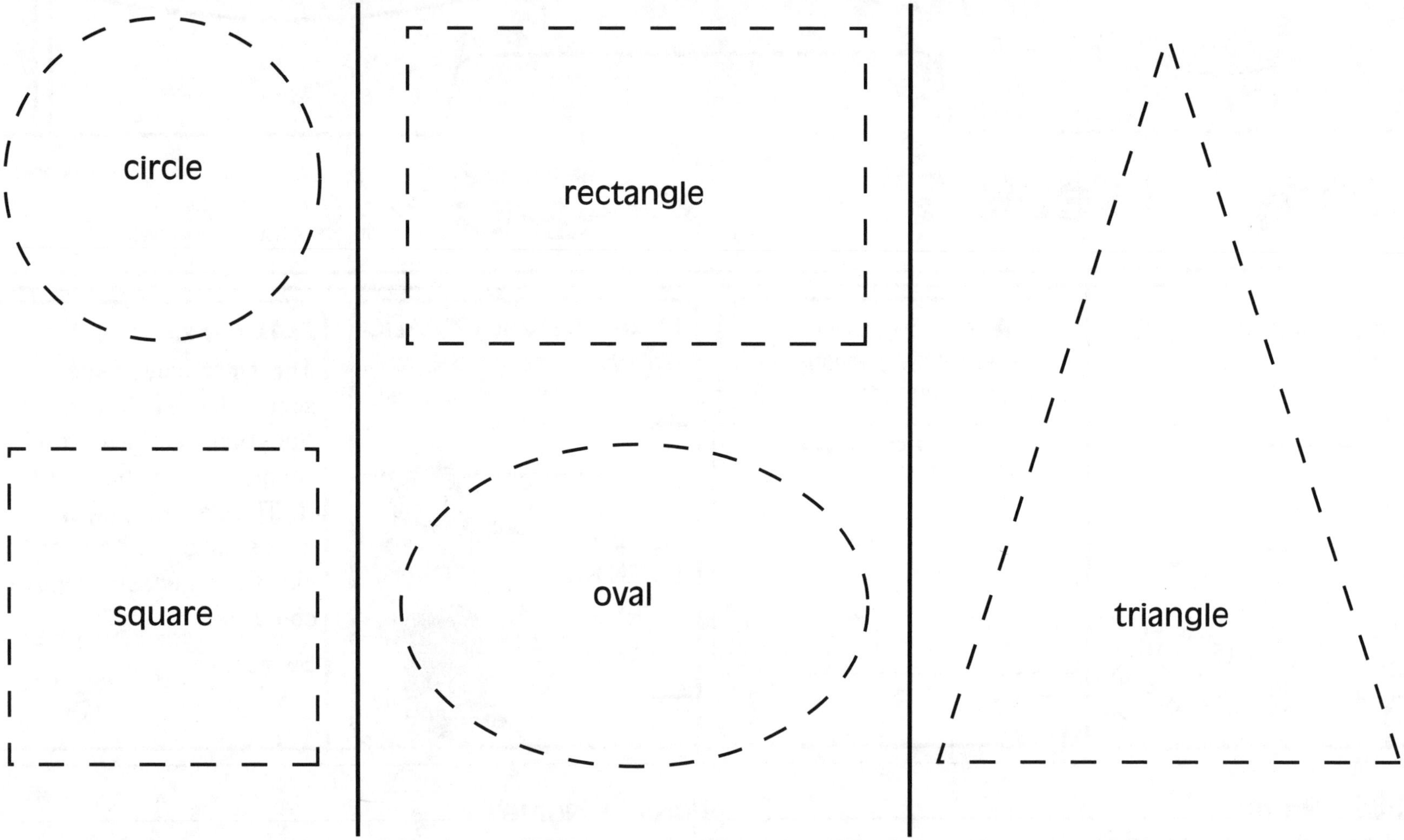

circle

rectangle

triangle

square

oval

SHAPE-UP — Connect the dashes for each shape. Name the shapes you made.

On my LISTENING WALK
I heard:

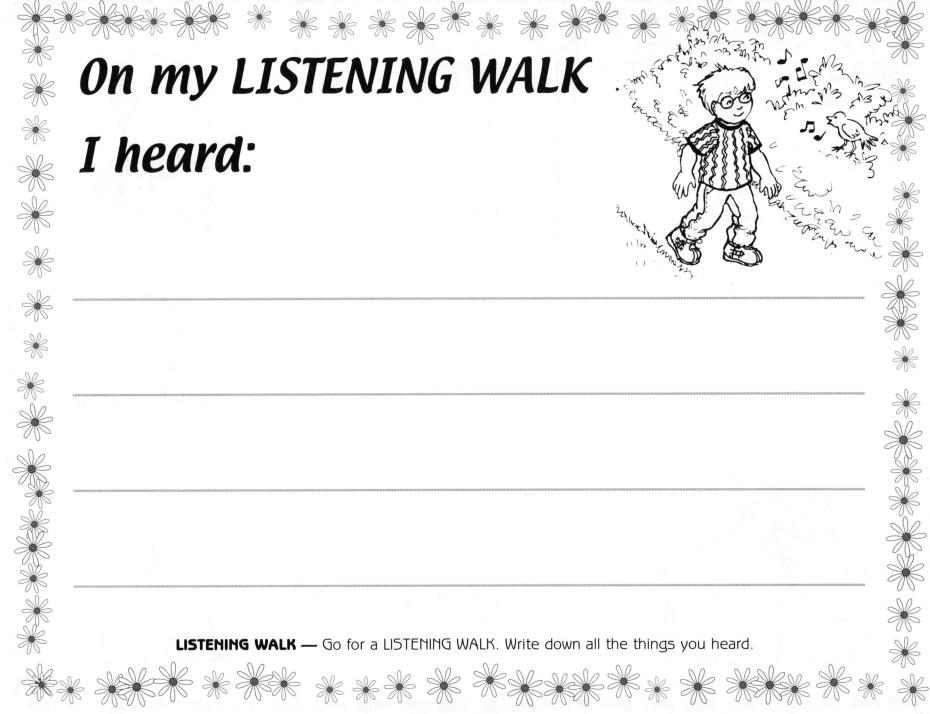

LISTENING WALK — Go for a LISTENING WALK. Write down all the things you heard.

SIDEWALK CHALK

Supplies

- Styrofoam cups
- Plaster of Paris
- Molds, such as:
- 🖉 Small dixie cups
- 🖉 Plastic popsicle molds
- 🖉 Small plastic cups from puddings, yogurt, etc.
- Sturdy mixing spoon
- Food coloring *(optional)*
- Water

Make SIDEWALK CHALK

1. Fill the styrofoam cup about 3/4 full of plaster.

2. Add food coloring to a 1/2 cup of water.

3. Slowly add the water to the plaster, stirring the whole time. Continue adding water until the mixture is that of cake batter. *(Use more or less water as needed.)*

4. Pour the mixture into the mold(s). Let the mold set for 2 hours or until the mixture hardens.

5. POP OUT YOUR NEW CHALK!!

Use SIDEWALK CHALK
Use it outside and inside. Especially fun on sidewalks and dark paper.

Store SIDEWALK CHALK
Put in a recloseable bag or a bucket with a lid. Easy to carry outside.

On Track To FIRST GRADE

June ~ Week 1

Have someone read to you.

Tell someone about your favorite character.

Find 2 things that feel:

_____ Soft

_____ Hard

_____ Bumpy or rough

_____ Smooth

Play **BASEBALL.**

Make **JUICE POPS.**

What kind did you make?

_____

Have Mom or Dad draw around your body while you lie on the sidewalk. Add your:

_____ Hair   _____ Ears

_____ Eyes   _____ Nose

_____ Mouth   _____ Clothes

_____ Shoes

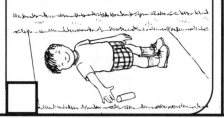

Child's Name _____   **Parent's Name** _____

www.bblocksonline.com

89

JUICE POPS

(Great Snack On a Warm Day!)

You'll Need

One of your child's favorite juices, such as:

Pineapple

Grape

Cranberry

Popsicle sticks

Small paper cups

Small eatable treat, such as raisins or grapes
(optional)

Make JUICE POPS

1. Fill the paper cups about 3/4 full of juice.

2. Put the cups in the freezer.

3. When the juice begins to freeze:

• Add the eatable treats *(optional)*.

• Put a popsicle stick in the middle of each cup at an angle.

4. Let freeze.

Eat Your JUICE POPS

Give each person a popsicle and let her wiggle it out of her cup. Keep the cups to catch the drips. On warm days enjoy them outside.

QUESTION OF THE WEEK

What is your Dad's name?

_____

How old is he?

_____

On Track To FIRST GRADE

June ~ Week 2

Have someone read to you.

Retell the story in your own words.

Tell someone 4 things you like to do.

swim, ride my bike...

On a big piece of paper draw and color a picture of you and your Dad doing something together.

Circle the Letters in Your Name	A	B	C	D	E
	a	b	c	d	e
F	G	H	I	J	K	L
f	g	h	i	j	k	l
M	N	O	P	Q	R	S
m	n	o	p	q	r	s
T	U	V	W	X	Y	Z
t	u	v	w	x	y	z

CIRCLE THE LETTERS IN YOUR NAME.

Count as high as you can.

How high did you count?

_____

1, 2, 3, 4, 5, 6, 7, 8, 9......

Child's Name _____

Parent's Name _____

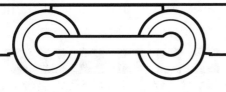

www.bblocksonline.com

91

Circle the Letters in Your Name

A **a**	**B** **b**	**C** **c**	**D** **d**	**E** **e**
F **f**	**G** **g**	**H** **h**	**I** **i**	**J** **j**	**K** **k**	**L** **l**
M **m**	**N** **n**	**O** **o**	**P** **p**	**Q** **q**	**R** **r**	**S** **s**
T **t**	**U** **u**	**V** **v**	**W** **w**	**X** **x**	**Y** **y**	**Z** **z**

CIRCLE THE LETTERS IN YOUR NAME — Find all the letters in your first and last name. Circle them. If your name has the same letter 2 or 3 times, circle it that many times.

QUESTION OF THE WEEK

How tall are you?

_____

On Track To FIRST GRADE

June ~ Week 3

Have someone read to you.

Are you like any of the characters in the story? Who? Why?

Write
your last name. How many letters are in it?

_____

Ford
4 letters

Sing
ON A PICNIC WE WILL GO.
Make a list of all your picnic items.

On a picnic we....

Put shaving cream on a cookie sheet. Use your pointer finger to make:

___ Letters   ___ Numbers

___ Shapes   ___ Pictures

___ Your name

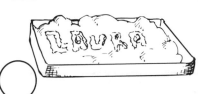

Play your favorite card game with your Mom or Dad.

Child's Name _____   **Parent's Name** _____

www.bblocksonline.com

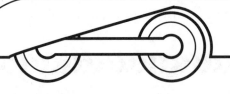

93

ON A PICNIC WE WILL GO

(tune: Farmer In the Dell)   by Liz Wilmes

On a picnic we will go.

On a picnic we will go.

Let's fill our basket up.

On a picnic we will go.

(Name) brings a _____.

(Name) brings a _____.

Let's fill our basket up.

On a picnic we will go.
(Continue with other people and picnic items.)

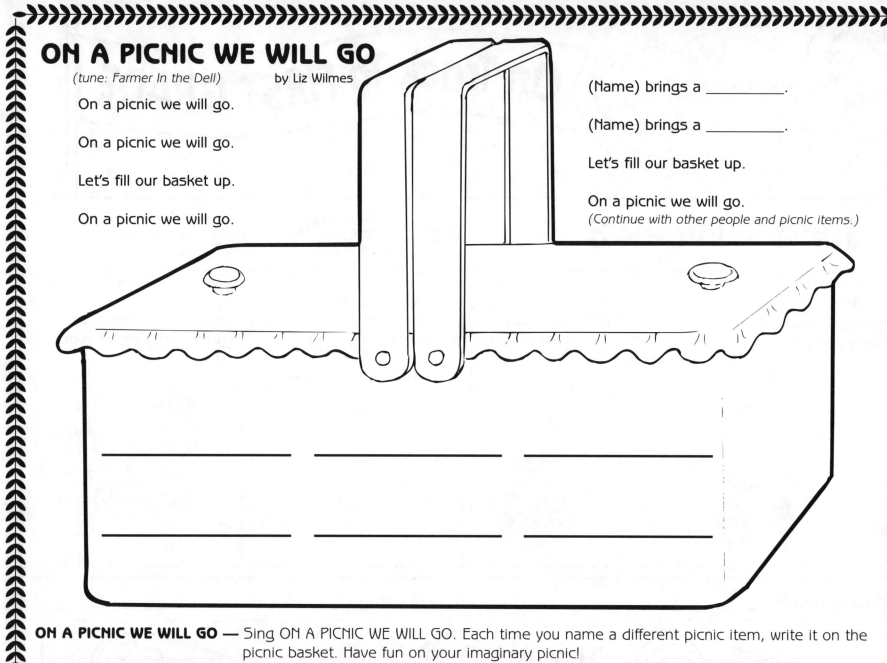

ON A PICNIC WE WILL GO — Sing ON A PICNIC WE WILL GO. Each time you name a different picnic item, write it on the picnic basket. Have fun on your imaginary picnic!

What do you want to be when you grow up?

_____

On Track To FIRST GRADE

June ~ Week 4

Before reading, look at the front cover. What do you think the story will be about?

MY NAME

Write your whole name.

Have someone roll a ball to you and you kick it back.

Keep playing.

Fill a spray bottle with water and have fun spraying the sidewalk, grass, trees, etc.

Play **CHECKERS**

How many games did you play? _____

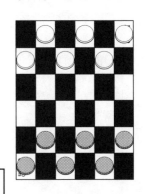

Child's Name _____ **Parent's Name** _____

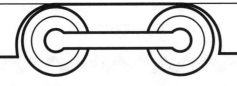  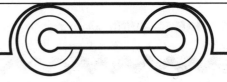

I can write my whole name.

I have _____ letters in my name.

MY NAME — Write your name. Count how many letters are in your name. Write the number down.

Checkers
Checkers

Checkers
Checkers

CHECKERS — Get 6 each of 2 different colored checkers or bottle caps. Using this small game board, play checkers in the traditional way.

www.bblocksonline.com

97

My Summer Journal

by _____

I went:

___ To the zoo

___ To a playground

___ To a park

___ To the beach

___ To a farm

___ To a museum

___ To the store

___ To an amusement park

___ To my grandparent's house

___ To a fireworks display

___ To the library

Add other places you went

Write about the places you went.

_____

_____

_____

_____

_____

_____

_____

I went:

___ Swimming

___ Camping

___ Boating or canoeing

___ Horseback riding

___ Bike riding

___ On a nature walk

___ Hiking

___ On a picnic

Add other things you did

_____ _____

_____ _____

_____ _____

Write or draw a picture about your favorite thing to do.

I played:

___ Tag

___ Hopscotch

___ Jumprope

___ Catch

___ With a Hula hoop

___ Hide and seek

___ Monkey in the middle

___ Baseball

___ Basketball

___ Soccer

Add other games you played

_____ _____

_____ _____

_____ _____

Write about a game you liked to play.

_____

_____

_____

_____

_____

_____

_____

I read a book about:

__ Bugs

__ Bears

__ Dinosaurs

__ Fish

__ Sharks

__ Whales

__ Dolphins

__ Dogs

__ Cats

Add your own

_____ _____

_____ _____

_____ _____

Write or draw a picture about one of the books you really liked.

I tried new things:

I learned new things:

I played with:

__ My sister

__ My brother

__ My mom/dad

Add other people you played with

_____

_____

_____

I played with my toys:

__ Blocks

__ Ball

__ Doll

__ Teddy bear

__ Puzzle

Add other toys you played with

_____

_____

_____

Draw a picture of yourself playing with someone.

Songs and Rhymes

ABC SONG

A, B, C, D, E, F, G

H, I, J, K, L, M , N, O, P,

Q, R, S, and

T, U, V,

W, X, Y, and Z.

... sing with me!

Now I've said my A B C's
Next time won't
You sing with me!

ARE YOU SLEEPING?

Are you sleeping?

Are you sleeping?

Brother John,

Brother John.

Morning bells are ringing.

Morning bells are ringing.

Ding, ding, dong.

Ding, ding, dong.

JOHNNY WORKS WITH ONE HAMMER

Johnny works with one hammer,
("Hammer" with 1 fist.)
One hammer, one hammer.
Johnny works with one hammer,
Now he works with 2.
("Hammer" with 2 fists.)

Johnny works with two hammers,
Two hammers, two hammers.
Johnny works with two hammers,
Now he works with 3.
("Hammer" with 2 fists and 1 foot.)

Johnny works with three hammers,
Three hammers, three hammers.
Johnny works with three hammers,
Now he works with 4.
("Hammer" with 2 fists and 2 feet.)

Johnny works with four hammers,
Four hammers, four hammers.
Johnny works with four hammers,
Now he works with 5.
("Hammer with 2 fists, 2 feet, and head.)

Johnny works with five hammers,
Five hammers, five hammers.
Johnny works with five hammers,
Now he goes to sleep. (Lie down.)

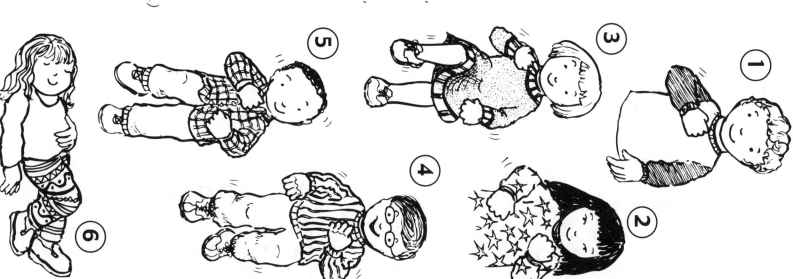

1 LITTLE, 2 LITTLE, 3 LITTLE HEARTS

1 little, 2 little, 3 little hearts,

(Put up fingers as you sing.)

4 little, 5 little, 6 little hearts,

7 little, 8 little, 9 little hearts,

Bring love on VALENTINE'S DAY.

1, 2, 3 THERE'S A BUG ON ME

1

2

3

There's a bug on me.

Where did he go?

I don't know.
(Shrug shoulders.)

TWINKLE, TWINKLE LITTLE STAR

Twinkle, twinkle little star

How I wonder what you are.

Up above the world so high,

Like a diamond in the sky.

WE EAT TURKEY

(tune: Are You Sleeping)

We eat turkey, we eat turkey
Oh so good, oh so good.

Always on Thanksgiving,
Always on Thanksgiving.

Yum, yum, yum,
Yum, yum, yum!

We eat...

(Continue singing,
letting your child add foods.)

by Liz Wilmes

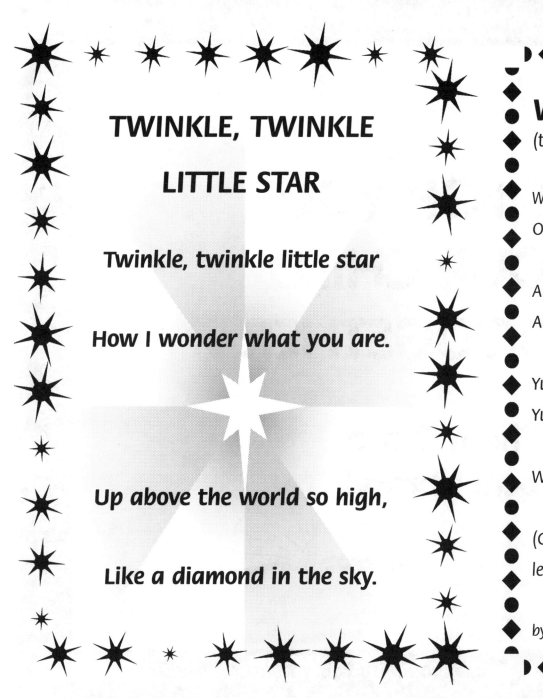

BOOKS FOR YOU
AND YOUR CHILD
TO READ TOGETHER

Check Them Out at
Your Local Library!

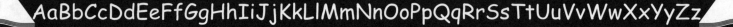

ALEXANDER AND THE TERRIBLE, HORRIBLE, NO GOOD, VERY BAD DAY
by Judith Viorst

ANIMALS SHOULD DEFINITELY NOT WEAR CLOTHING
by Judi Barrett

BEARY MORE
by Don Freeman

BLUEBERRIES FOR SAL
by Robert McCloskey

BOOK! BOOK! BOOK!
by Deborah Brass

THE BOSSY GALLITO: A TRADITIONAL CUBAN FOLK TALE
retold by Lucia M.Gonzalez

BREAD AND JAM FOR FRANCES
by Russell Hoban

BROWN BEAR, BROWN BEAR, WHAT DO YOU SEE
by Bill Martin, Jr.

CAPS FOR SALE: A TALE OF A PEDDLER, SOME MONKEYS AND THEIR MONKEY BUSINESS
by Esphty Slobodkina

THE CARROT SEED
by Ruth Krauss

THE CHAIR FOR MY MOTHER
by Vera B. Williams

CHICKA CHICKA BOOM BOOM
by Bill Martin, Jr. and John Archambault

CHICKEN SOUP WITH RICE
by Maurice Sendak

CHRYSANTHEMUM
by Kevin Henkes

CORDUROY
by Don Freeman

COME ALONG, DAISY
by Jane Simmons

CURIOUS GEORGE
by H.A. Rey

CURIOUS GEORGE MAKES PANCAKES
by H.A. Rey

THE DAY JIMMY BOA ATE THE WASH
by Trinka H. Noble

DOCTOR DE SOTO
by William Steig

THE DOORBELL RANG
by Pat Hutchins

EATING THE ALPHABET: FRUITS AND VEGETABLES FROM A TO Z
by Lois Ehlert

EMILY'S FIRST 100 DAYS OF SCHOOL
by Rosemary Wells

FREIGHT TRAIN
by Donald Crews

GEORGE AND MARTHA
by James Marshall

GINGERBREAD BABY
by Jan Brett

GO AWAY, BIG GREEN MONSTER!
by Ed Emberly

GOOD NIGHT, GORILLA
by Peggy Rathmann

GOODNIGHT MOON
by Margaret W. Brown

GROWING VEGETABLE SOUP
by Lois Ehlert

HAPPY BIRTHDAY, MOON
by Frank Asch

HAROLD AND THE PURPLE CRAYON
by Crockett Johnson

HARRY THE DIRTY DOG
by Gene Zion

THE HAT
by Jan Brett

HENNY PENNY
illustrated Paul Galdone

HORTON HATCHES THE EGG
by Dr. Seuss

I KNOW AN OLD LADY WHO SWALLOWED A FLY
illustrated Glen Rounds

IF YOU GIVE A MOUSE A COOKIE
by Laura J. Numeroff

IN THE TALL, TALL GRASS
by Denise Fleming

JESSICA
by Kevin Henkes

JULIUS
by Angela Johnson

KOALA LOU
by Mem Fox

KISSING HAND
by Audrey Penn

LEO THE LATE BLOOMER
by Robert Kraus

THE LITTLE DOG LAUGHED AND OTHER NURSERY RHYMES
by Lucy Cousins

THE LITTLE MOUSE, THE RED STRAWBERRY, AND THE BIG HUNGRY BEAR
by Don and Audrey Wood

LITTLE RED RIDING HOOD
retold and illustrated by Paul Galdone

LYLE, LYLE CROCODILE
by Bernard Waber

MADELINE
by Ludwig Bemelmans

MAISIE GOES SWIMMING
by Lucy Cousins

MAKE WAY FOR DUCKLINGS
by Robert McCloskey

MARY WORE HER RED DRESS and HENRY WORE HIS GREEN SNEAKERS
by Merle Peek

MIKE MULLIGAN AND HIS STEAM SHOVEL
by Virginia L. Burton

MILLIONS OF CATS
by Wanda Gag

MISS BINDERGARTEN GETS READY FOR KINDERGARTEN
by Joseph Slate

MISS BINDERGARTEN TAKES A FIELD TRIP WITH KINDERGARTEN
  by Joseph Slate

MISS SPIDER'S TEA PARTY
  by Edith Patton

MRS. SPITZER'S GARDEN
  by Edith Patton

THE MITTEN
  by Jan Brett

THE NAPPING HOUSE
  by Audrey Wood

OFFICER BUCKLE AND GLORIA
  by Peggy Rathmann

OWEN
  by Kevin Henkes

OWL BABIES
  by Martin Waddell

PANCAKES FOR BREAKFAST
  by Tomie De Paola

PETE'S A PIZZA
  by William Steig

THE PICKY EATER
  by Marc Brown

THE RAINBOW FISH
  by Marcus Pfister

ROSIE'S WALK
  by Pat Hutchins

RUNAWAY BUNNY
  Margaret Wise Brown

THE SNOWY DAY
   by Ezra Jack Keats

SWIMMY
  by Leo Lionni

THERE'S A NIGHTMARE IN MY CLOSET
  by Mercer Mayer

TIMOTHY GOES TO SCHOOL
   by Rosemary Wells

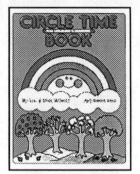

B U I L D I N G B L O C K S Library

CIRCLE TIME SERIES

by *Liz & Dick Wilmes*. **Thousands of activities for large and small groups of children. Each book is filled with Language and Active games, Fingerplays, Songs, Stories, Snacks, and more. A great resource for every library shelf.**

Circle Time Book
Captures the spirit of 39 holidays and seasons
ISBN 0-943452-00-7 . . . .$12.95

Everyday Circle Times
Over 900 ideas. Choose from 48 topics divided into 7 sections: self-concept, basic concepts, animals, foods, science, occupations, and recreation.
ISBN 0-943452-01-5 . . . .$16.95

More Everyday Circle Times
Divided into the same 7 sections as EVERYDAY. Features new topics such as Birds and Pizza, plus all new ideas for some of the popular topics contained in EVERYDAY.
ISBN 0-943452-14-7 . . . .$16.95

Yearful of Circle Times
52 different topics to use weekly, by seasons, or mixed throughout the year. New Friends, Signs of Fall, Snowfolk Fun, and much more.
ISBN 0-943452-10-4 . . . .$16.95

ART

Paint Without Brushes
by *Liz & Dick Wilmes*. Use common materials which you already have. Discover the painting possibilities in your classroom! PAINT WITHOUT BRUSHES gives your children open-ended art activities to explore paint in lots of creative ways. A valuable art resource. One you'll want to use daily.
ISBN 0-943452-15-5 . . . .$12.95

Easel Art
by *Liz & Dick Wilmes*. Let the children use easels, walls, outside fences, clip boards, and more as they enjoy the variety of art activities filling the pages of EASEL ART. A great book to expand young children's art experiences.
ISBN 0-943452-25-2 . . . .$12.95

Everyday Bulletin Boards
by *Wilmes and Moehling*. Features borders, murals, backgrounds, and other open-ended art to display on your bulletin boards. Plus board ideas with patterns, which teachers can make and use to enhance their curriculum.
ISBN 0-943452-09-0 . . . .$12.95

Exploring Art
by *Liz & Dick Wilmes*. EXPLORING ART is divided by months. Over 250 art ideas for paint, chalk, doughs, scissors, and more. Easy to set-up in your classroom.
ISBN 0-943452-05-8 . . . .$19.95

LEARNING GAMES & ACTIVITIES

Magnet Board Fun
by Liz & Dick Wilmes Every classroom has a magnet board, every home a refrigerator. MAGNET BOARD FUN is crammed full of games, songs, and stories. Hundreds of patterns to reproduce, color, and use immediately.
ISBN 0-943452-28-7 . . . .$16.95

Table & Floor Games
by Liz & Dick Wilmes. 32 easy-to-make, fun-to-play table/floor games with accompanying patterns ready to duplicate. Teach beginning concepts such as matching, counting, colors, alphabet, and so on.
ISBN 0-943452-16-3 . . . .$19.95

Activities Unlimited
by Adler, Caton, and Cleveland. Hundreds of innovative activities to develop fine and gross motor skills, increase language, become self-reliant, and play cooperatively. This book will quickly become a favorite.
ISBN 0-943452-17-1 . . . .$16.95

Learning Centers
by Liz & Dick Wilmes. Hundreds of open-ended activities to quickly involve and excite your children. You'll use it every time you plan and whenever you need a quick, additional activity. A must for every teacher's bookshelf.
ISBN 0-943452-13-9 . . . .$19.95

Games for All Seasons
by Caton and Cleveland Play with the wonder of seasons and holidays. Use acorns, pumpkins, be clouds and butterflies, go ice fishing. Over 150 learning games.
ISBN 0-943452-29-5 . . . .$16.95

Play With Big Boxes
by Liz & Dick Wilmes. Children love big boxes. Turn them into boats, telephone booths, tents, and other play areas. Bring them to art and let children collage, build, and paint them. Use them in learning centers for games, play stages, quiet spaces, puzzles, and more, more, more.
ISBN 0-943452-23-6 . . . .$12.95

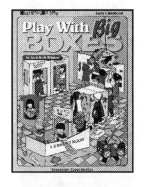

Felt Board Fingerplays
by Liz & Dick Wilmes. A year full of fingerplay fun. Over 50 popular fingerplays with full-size patterns. All accompanied by games and activities.
ISBN 0-943452-26-0 . . . .$16.95

Play With Small Boxes
by Liz & Dick Wilmes. Small boxes are free, fun, and unlimited. Use them for telephones, skates, scoops, pails, doll beds, buggies, and more. So many easy activities, you'll use small boxes every day.
ISBN 0-943452-24-4 . . . .$12.95

Felt Board Fun
by Liz & Dick Wilmes. Make your felt board come alive. This unique book has over 150 ideas with patterns.
ISBN 0-943452-02-3 . . . .$16.95

Parachute Play, Revised
by Liz & Dick Wilmes. Play, wiggle, and laugh as you introduce children to the parachute. Over 150 holiday and everyday games for inside and outside play.
ISBN 0-943452-30-9 . . . .$12.95

Felt Board Stories
by Liz & Dick Wilmes. 25 seasonal, holiday, and any-day stories with full-size patterns. Children are involved in each story. They figure out riddles, create endings, sing with characters, add patterns, and so much more.
ISBN 0-945452-31-7 . . . .$16.95

"ON TRACK" Series

by Alex Cleveland & Barb Caton

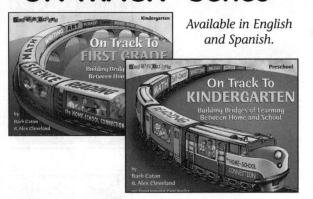

Available in English and Spanish.

Make the HOME-SCHOOL CONNECTION!
Parents ask, *"How can I help my child get ready for kindergarten? What can I do to help my child succeed in first grade?"*

Answer: These books are the answer! The Weekly Activity Sheets are filled with games and activities that parents can do with their children.

ISBN 0-943452-32-5 (Kindergarten, English) $14.95

ISBN 0-943452-33-3 (Kindergarten, Spanish) $14.95

ISBN 0-943452-34-1 (First Grade, English) $14.95

ISBN 0-943452-35-X (First Grade, Spanish) $14.95

2's Experience Series

by Liz and Dick Wilmes. An exciting series developed especially for toddlers and twos!

2's-Art
Scribble, Paint, Smear, Mix , Tear, Mold, Taste, and more. Over 150 activities, plus lots of recipes and hints.
ISBN 0-943452-21-X $16.95

2's-Sensory Play
Hundreds of playful, multi-sensory activities to encourage children to look, listen, taste, touch, and smell.
ISBN 0-943452-22-8 . . . . $14.95

2's-Dramatic Play
Dress up and pretend! Hundreds of imaginary situations and settings.
ISBN 0-943452-20-1 . . . . $12.95

2's-Stories
Excite children with story books! Read—Expand the stories with games, songs, and rhymes. Over 40 books with patterns.
ISBN 0-943452-27-9 . . . . $16.95

2's-Fingerplays
A wonderful collection of easy fingerplays with accompanying games and large FINGERPLAY CARDS.
ISBN 0-943452-18-X $12.95

2's-Felt Board Fun
Make your felt board come alive. Enjoy stories, activities, and rhymes. Hundreds of extra large patterns.
ISBN 0-943452-19-8 . . . . $14.95

BUILDING BLOCKS

BUILDING BLOCKS Subscription $20.00

CIRCLE TIME Series
CIRCLE TIME BOOK 12.95
EVERYDAY CIRCLE TIMES 16.95
MORE EVERYDAY CIRCLE TIMES 16.95
YEARFUL OF CIRCLE TIMES 16.95

ART
EASEL ART 12.95
EVERYDAY BULLETIN BOARDS 12.95
EXPLORING ART 19.95
PAINT WITHOUT BRUSHES 12.95

LEARNING GAMES & ACTIVITIES
ACTIVITIES UNLIMITED 16.95
FELT BOARD FINGERPLAYS 16.95
FELT BOARD FUN 16.95
FELT BOARD STORIES 16.95
LEARNING CENTERS 19.95
MAGNET BOARD FUN 16.95
PARACHUTE PLAY, REVISED 12.95
PLAY WITH BIG BOXES 12.95
PLAY WITH SMALL BOXES 12.95
TABLE & FLOOR GAMES 19.95

ON TRACK SERIES
ON TRACK TO KINDERGARTEN (ENGLISH) . . . 14.95
ON TRACK TO KINDERGARTEN (SPANISH) . . . 14.95
ON TRACK TO FIRST GRADE (ENGLISH) 14.95
ON TRACK TO FIRST GRADE (SPANISH) 14.95

2's EXPERIENCE Series
2'S EXPERIENCE - ART 16.95
2'S EXPERIENCE - DRAMATIC PLAY 12.95
2'S EXPERIENCE - FELTBOARD FUN 14.95
2'S EXPERIENCE - FINGERPLAYS 12.95
2'S EXPERIENCE - SENSORY PLAY 14.95
2'S EXPERIENCE - STORIES 16.95

Prices subject to change without notice.

All books available from full-service book stores, educational stores, and school supply catalogs.

Check Our Website: **www.bblocksonline.com**